RIVER FRIEND

A series of Riverine Small Books

by Sylvia M. Haslam and Tina Bone

BOOK 1

DRYING UP

Book 1

DRYING UP

A Book in a series of Riverine
publications by

Sylvia M. Haslam and Tina Bone

*Written and Edited by Sylvia Haslam and
Tina Bone. Illustrated by Tina Bone
(unless otherwise stated)*

RFS1: PAPERBACK 40pp.
ISBN No. 978 1 9162096 1 9
35 Illustrations

Published by: Tina Bone UK
First edition: September 2019
Revision 1: December 2019
Revision 2: March 2020
Revision 3: June 2020
www.riverfriend.tinasfineart.uk

CONTENTS

INTRODUCTION TO THE SERIES

Rivers are vital. They bring freshwater to the land, on which all its life depends. They are beautiful and fascinating, making up both the typical British countryside and many of its most spectacular views. If they vanished, what hardship and outrage there would be! Yet, slowly, slowly, they are vanishing, the larger stream becomes smaller, the tiny brook becomes a ditch and dries, and is filled in— the small ditches get polluted and dug out, become dull, and vanish from sight and consciousness. How can we save our rivers and riverscapes? How can we raise awareness on this slow, almost invisible loss?

We believe that this series of handy, small books, suitable for readers from teenage upwards, will help to raise awareness. Individually, each book tells a story on a particular riverine and riparian environment. Collectively, the series will inform, in a simple and effective manner, the invaluable worth of freshwater and its plants.

The Authors realised that there was a huge gap in the literature. There are many publications for scientists, for pond-dippers, birders and anglers, but "easy-read" books focussing on the river itself, and the vegetation belonging to it and creating the habitat for all else: we could find none!

For explanations regarding British freshwater plants, terminology mentioned throughout the series, and Picture Guide and reference section for further reading, see the book entitled *A PROLOGUE TO THE SERIES: Plant identification and Glossary of Terms* (also available to view free on-line at http://riverfriend.tinasfineart.uk/product/a-prologue-to-the-river-friend-series-isbn-978-1-9162096-2-6/)

Other titles in the Series are listed on the last page of this book and on the River Friend Website:
http://www.riverfriend.tinasfineart.uk

DRYING UP

Introduction

What is the worst that can happen to a river? That it vanishes, and all its life vanishes with it: the people, the plants, the animals—not just the fish, but the crops, the cattle, the forests, the everything. All are made mostly of water. Look around—what is in that leaf, that spider, that deer, that petal?—WATER! And although many animals and (mostly tiny) plants live in the sea in salt water, it is the fresh water in the land, derived from rain, which supports us and our main natural resources.

This series of books takes different aspects of rivers and begins to explain each. There is little overlap: *WATER: Clean and Dirty* deals with pollution. Pollution occurs in the River Brue, but in its book the focus is in the development and changes of that river—pollution being incidental. And so on.

For most of human history, on most of the land, there has been sufficient, ample, or too much water. Excess water means flooded land, with all that that entails of damage to life and property. It means saturated soils in the wet or rainy season, so (until recent technology) rheumatics or arthritis and a whole show of damp-enhanced diseases: of people, livestock and crops. As population increases, so people want more water. Livestock (whose numbers have dramatically **increased** to serve increased demand) may do so also, but in view of the enormous herds of wild animals formerly (whose numbers have **decreased**), it is difficult to say water demand *here* has increased. But when water has to be carried into houses, that is inconvenient and heavy! Stop for a few moments and think what you, the Reader, would not do if you had to carry water in.

The worst threat to our environment is from the loss of fresh water, even when compared with the loss of rain forests, climate change, and air pollution. Without water, ALL LIFE disappears.

But, surely water can not disappear? The molecules of Hydrogen and Oxygen (H_2O) are indestructible. True. Water flows from land to sea, it evaporates into the sky and falls to the land again as rain—a continuous process. So what is wrong with that? It is wrong when the "process" is interrupted by people removing water from the land for many reasons and therefore much less of the total supply is on or under the land and all that the land bears. Much more is in the sea, where it does us little good.

This is rather difficult to grasp, given the British floods of the early twenty-first century. Too much water on the land, surely? But for every acre flooded, for a few weeks (seldom for months nowadays!) there are many which are drier than a couple of centuries ago.

Over the millions of years that plants and animals have inhabited the earth, climate has changed, hotter, colder, drier, wetter, and—slowly, slowly—plants and animals have evolved and changed to adapt to these changes. Here, though, we are concerned only with recent, escalating developments: primarily causative man-made changes.

Water Usage

Running-water taps are convenient and increase usage. Hot-water taps increase it more, and inexpensive dishwashers and washing machines increase it still more—laundry may be done daily or twice daily rather than weekly or fortnightly. So water demand for people increases with both total population and urbanisation/technology. General research shows that in 2019 it has reached 150 litres per person per day or even more in Britain, and 250 litres or so in the USA.

Water on land has vastly decreased. How does that come about? For centuries passage for boats has been made easier by cutting off bends in waterways (Fig. 1): technically, removing meanders, clearing ox-bow lakes which, in the course of time, dry, or are drained. Secondly, with improved technology, river courses have been canalised, narrowed and deepened (Fig. 2).

This means more riverside land can be used (for instance, for pasture, woodland or crops). The differences overall in land taken up, and so reduced water habitat, is considerable: shallow rivers with gravelly or mixed substrata can have plenty of fauna and vegetation—although deep water (75cm–1.75m deep), unless very clear and clean, does not have much vegetation because not enough light reaches the bottom.

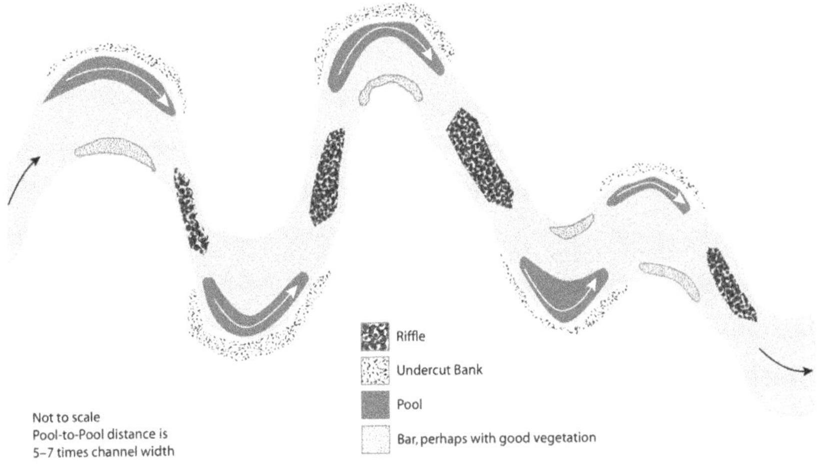

Fig. 1a. Meander Development. Pool and riffle pattern

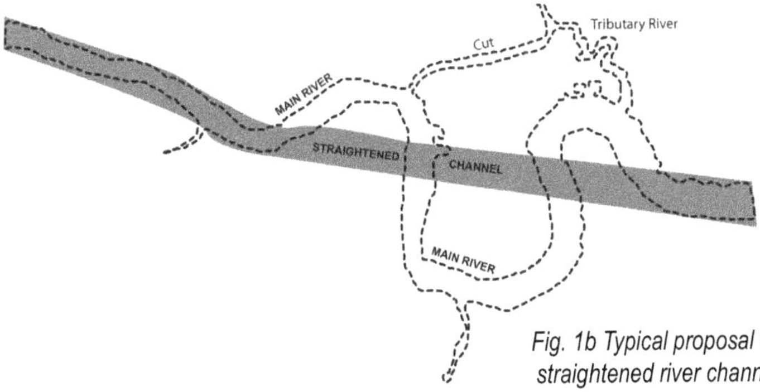

*Fig. 1b Typical proposal for
straightened river channel*

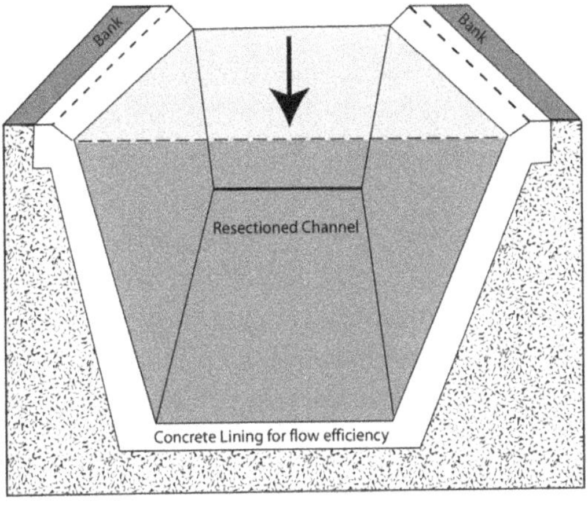

*Fig. 2. A resectioned channel.
Compare habitat diversity and
quality with a more natural
channel as in Fig. 3a*

People and crops need water. In fact, great though the amount of water wanted by people is, these days crops require even more. It is surprising that when crop varieties have been bred for so many different features such as increased yield, increased starch or sugar or disease resistance, proportionately little effort goes into making them drought-tolerant so that less water is needed. It is timely that trials were carried out in 2019 by the National Farmers Union in the UK under the Drought Risk and You (DRY) Project, funded by the Natural Environment Research Council as part of its UK Droughts and Water Scarcity programme (NERC 2019. Updates: http://dryproject.co.uk).

Abstraction and Drainage Systems

Water is taken from surface water stores, rills, streams, rivers, lakes and underground water stores (sometimes flooded caves, more often in saturated porous rock, especially limestone, sandstone, and in peats and marshes). All this abstraction lowers total water level.

Water level is also often lowered for the sake of drying the ground. People suffer from nasty diseases in damp houses, built on damp ground. So do crops. Both have a fairly narrow tolerance range of the dampness they need, though this does vary. For instance, rice needs much water, wheat some water, and olives only a little. So when conditions and technology allow, the dampness of the soil is adapted to be good for each crop and for people. Obviously there are places with little natural dampness, for example, arid areas and deserts, and places with much dampness, high rainfall, with the water collecting by gravity in hollows and peat-making areas. By and large, most good agricultural land used to be wet, but is now much drier.

Both above and below ground level much water has been removed for various reasons. Above-ground streams have dried with persistent drainage. Figure 3a shows a typical undrained stream which could be anywhere over a large part of (undrained) Europe. This stream is undrained, typically because it is in woodland and therefore with no economic or agricultural need to drain it. (If upstream it had flowed through agricultural land, it probably would have been drained.) Note the size, shape, and the good vegetation. Figure 3b, situated barely half a mile from Figure 3a, a stream surrounded by agricultural land, *is* drained. The difference is stark. The ground water level is much lower: the upper soil has less water. The aquatic habitat is much less and mostly too shallow for water-supported species, and the steep banks and hedges shade the water. From a good and diverse flora and fauna viewpoint, the channel has deteriorated greatly! And the stream *is still there*!

Fig. 3a. Oligotrophic forest stream, Norway, with little management, Resistant rock, south Norway. Species include Potamogeton polygonifolius, Glyceria fluitans *(long-leaved form),* Sparganium emersum, Alisma plantago-aquatica, Sparganium erectum, Ranunculus flammula *and* Luzula sylvatica. *Re-drawn from Haslam, 1987*

Fig. 3b. Small, narrow, steep-sided streams in grassland, often within tree-bands. Resistant rock, south Norway. Macrophytes absent. Re-drawn from Haslam, 1987

Figure 4 shows a typical (English) surface drainage progression. The top figure (from aerial photography) shows the original stream meandering down a gentle slope. The middle figure shows when (small) fields were constructed, ditches and hedges were put round each field, the water being able to move down to the rivers in the valley, and the fields being substantially drier. The next stage, bottom figure, is when the ditches have dried, so are no longer needed, except for the sparse ones now taking water downhill and into the main stream in the valley bottom.

This is surface draining of the land. But together with this there has been draining underground—under-drainage. This is easy to overlook, as it is unseen. But walking along the banks of streams it is often possible to see, as shown in Figure 5a–d. Drainage, loss of streams.

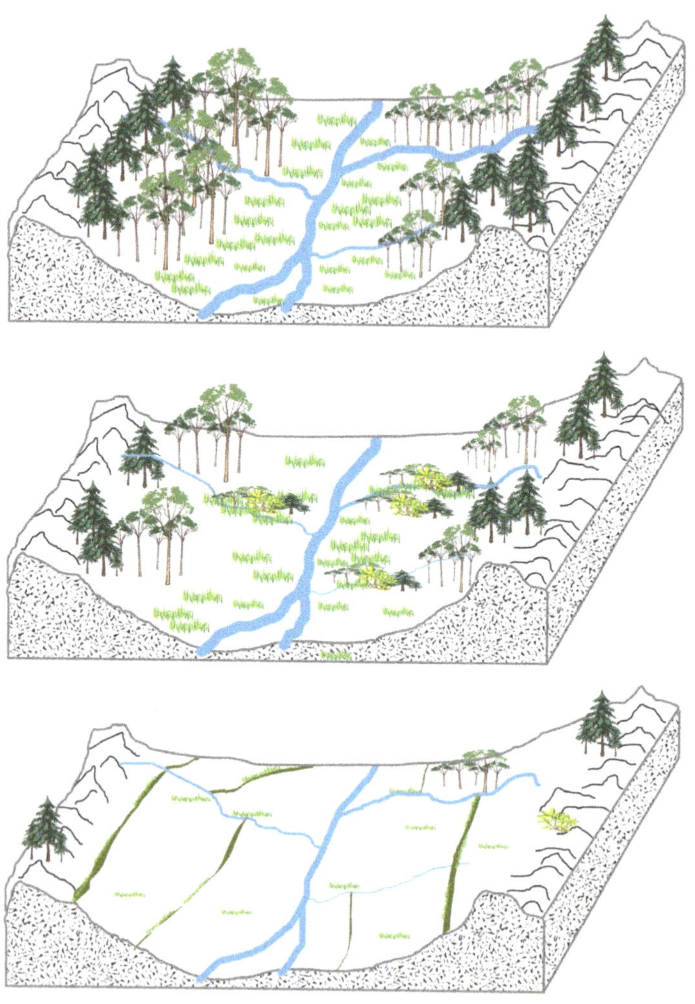

Fig. 4. Typical surface drainage progression—UK

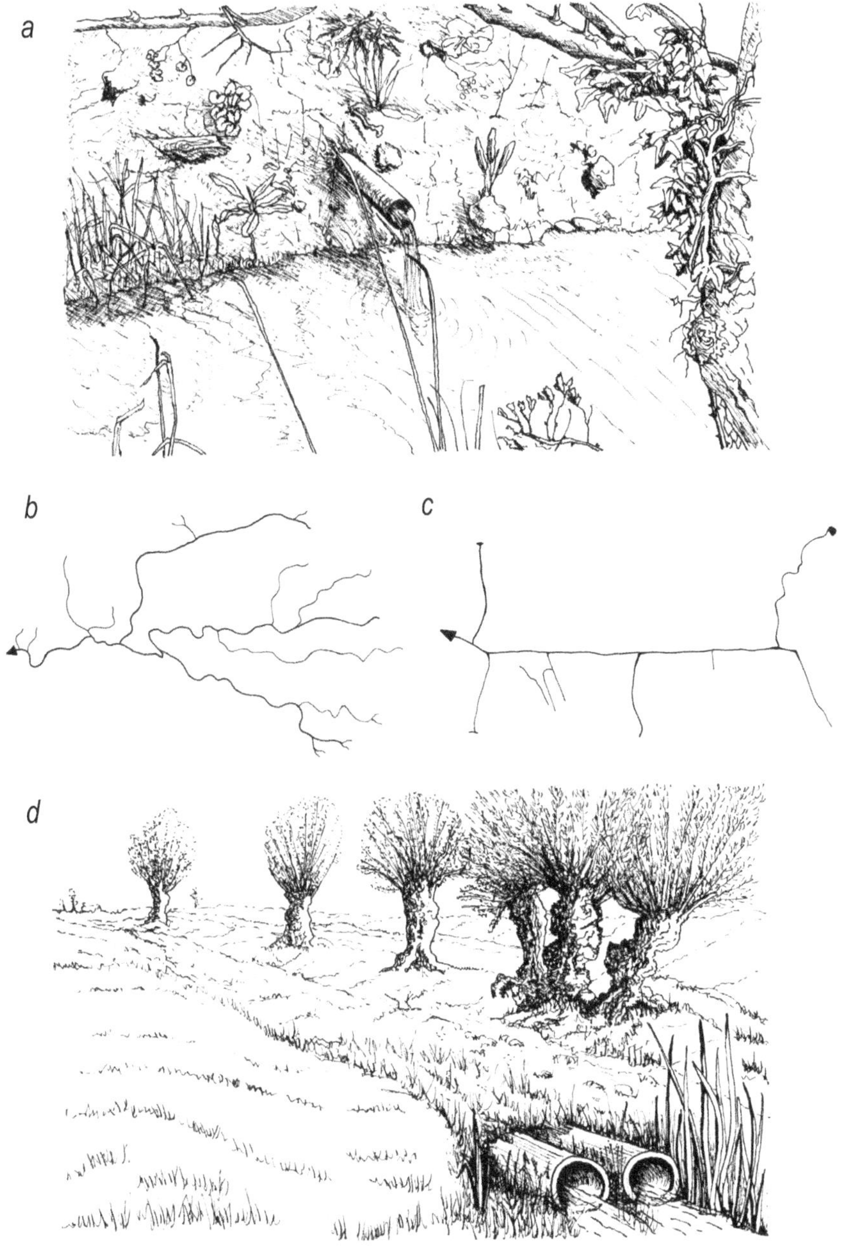

Fig. 5. Drainage, loss of streams

Fig. 5a. Typical under-drainage pipe draining into brook from arable fields. Fig. 5b. Typical undrained streams pattern; Fig. 5c. Typical drained streams pattern; Fig. 5d. Piped and "lost" tributary

Pipes may be well covered and intermittently discharge into streams from (non-steep) land above. Pipes like this in built-up areas, near roads, etc., are more properly "sewers", carrying road or building runoff, or worse. But from fields, they are under-drains or of course "proper" streams which have been put underground. These also are very efficient at lowering ground water level.

Given the same rainfall, the quicker it runs off to a river, the drier the land, so there is less aquatic habitat. Look again at Figures 2 and 3. See how much water habitat—its own features and the flora and fauna it could potentially bear—has been lost to facilitate good crop production: loss even when "Set Aside" policies are in place to conserve the ecology. But how many look at the grassy buffer strip and see the flowers and flies, and how many look for the water? Sadly, not enough for aquatic conservation!

Consider the loss this means over large areas, over the agricultural and pastural parts of the countryside. The loss is incomprehensible! The length of stream and river today is probably less than half what it was in 1700, even in 1850. Certainly it is, by and large, the narrower channels that have gone, the wider channels, with more water habitat, are still with us: but look back at Figure 4, and reflect upon the loss.

Managing Obstructions to Water Flow

Over the past 200 years or so, many "obstructions" such as weirs, dams, sluices, locks, clyses (or clysts), groynes and stanches have been removed. These are all man-made obstructions to river flow, and were constructed in the past for various, mostly industrial, purposes. A clyse, for example, is western—a type of sluice; a stanch, is eastern—a double channel, one side with a lock for boats, the other usually with more rapid flow and perhaps a weir.

In order to easily maximise crop yield, obstructions to river flow were removed from large areas wherever possible in the later twentieth century. Not just the old weirs and dams in the river beds, but everything slowing flow down the land, thus slowing water reaching the river. This included removal of hedges, banks, ditches (dry), trees, ponds, fences and walls. Water flowing over or through the soil was enabled to flow faster, dry more—and be lost to the smaller streams. Eventually, flash floods and erosion in wet years, and drought in dry ones, showed this had gone too far. In the drier climate of the east (Britain), where drying had happened most anyway, this became particularly noticeable. So some "obstructions" had to be put back, enabling rainfall to stay longer on the land. Unfortunately, a "replacement" brook, stone wall, or pond, may functionally be a replacement, but may not be so ecologically or culturally.

Britain's river environment has been more drained (managed) than on the European continent because of its high population and relatively little farmland and with much interest in farming amongst the educated classes. So the water loss has relatively been greater. For instance, in Denmark there is a nice little (barely 2m wide) stream not much over 50–75cm deep, with low banks (*Cf.* Fig 3a: low drainage) which was, apparently, good fishing for sea trout! In a similar stream in England there might—or might not—be a few sticklebacks: loss of habitat!

Ponds of Village and Field

Tractors. What have tractors to do with the drying up of land and freshwater? A lot, in fact. During the twentieth century, tractors replaced ploughs pulled by horses (or oxen or men). We all know that tractors can work most or all of the day (ordinarily) without needing any attention. They do need oil (petrol, diesel, or earlier in a minor way, steam) and maintenance from time to time. This is, however, NEW. Pre-tractor, draught animals—and men—needed to drink. Horses, and other moving livestock needed much water. So they needed to drink during the day. This was so obvious it rarely appears in the general literature. Now, however, we need to ask where the water came from. Villages usually had village ponds where horses and cattle could drink (Fig. 6). So did

Fig. 6. Typical historical Village pond for watering of livestock, etc.

farms. (Travellers in carts, coaches or on horseback needed frequent watering places along roads. Cows and other livestock being moved, or loose in a village, might do so too.) Towns likewise made provision. Importantly for the aquatic habitat there were small ponds at the corners or sides of fields, plenty of them, as well as springs, which were also far more numerous when ground water level was higher. Then there were the more localised industrial pits of clay and lime, which often flooded once abandoned.

Fig. 7a. Ober Water, Hampshire. Not only does this show a lack of aquatic vegetation, there is also very little water

Fig. 7b. Ober Water further upstream. Much trampling, no vegetation and even less water than in Fig. 7a (Photographs taken 30th May 2019, courtesy of Lisa Bone)

In the 1950s, livestock ponds could still be seen in many fields. Any water that remains for a few days acquires micro-organisms and invertebrates. Vegetation needs damp, wet or water habitat for at least a few months: but it comes. If, though, there is constant trampling by livestock or other disturbance, proper vegetation is little or absent—see Figure 7a, b, taken in the New Forest, Hampshire May 2019. Birds can fly in, but fish need a means of escape—along a stream, for instance. By the early twenty-first century most ponds in field and village had disappeared and many of the fresh springs which fed these had ceased to flow, probably due to over-abstraction of the aquifer.

Slowing Water Flow

The type of vegetation on the land may be indirectly important in slowing down the flow of water (Fig. 8). Obviously it seldom has much effect on the rainfall (rain shadows—the dry area on the leeward side of a mountainous area, away from the wind—and aridity may do so). But rain that falls directly onto the ground reaches it more quickly than if it falls on leaves, and probably on more leaves, on its way to the ground. When heavy rain passes through thick vegetation and onto soil with good drainage, water level from that rain rises more slowly, so the storm flows are less deep, less fierce, and take longer to pass. Conversely, rain on land which falls directly onto surfaces it cannot sink into, creates sharp, deep, fierce flows, known (when severe) as "flash" floods or flows.

Fig. 8. There is much surface-water where rain falls on buildings and hard surfaces such as car parks; fields and grass allow more seepage; but trees slow down rainfall much more

In much of Britain (and other countries where the climate encourages forest growth) woodland is the traditional native vegetation, and so has the least storm or flash flows. Short vegetation, such as pasture or crops, has more (unless the land is carefully managed), and hard surface such as tarmac, has most runoff. These flash flows are fierce and strong and, on slopes particularly, have much power to erode the earth below. So stream beds are lowered, channels deepened, water levels are lowered, and less storm water stays in the stream (Fig. 9).

Lowering water level by decreasing water is of course removing water. But water level is also lowered by dredging, so deepening the bed and increasing bank height. It may be obvious which—or both—have occurred. Dredging and deepening remove the hard bed of the river which—if ground water level has dropped—may also mean river water loss.

Fig. 9. Stream pattern present, water mostly gone

Holding up flow creates slower, deeper water upstream. This may be just a short pool or it may last until the next obstruction upstream—"toe-to-tail" (Fig. 10). Clearly these obstructions hold up the water in the river! They may have been put in to collect fish into places from where they can be retrieved by nets and traps. They may also be to accumulate a head of water to turn a wheel for power in water mills or for river control and management.

Boats cannot pass through solid dams or weirs. They may be carried round these (portage) or the sluice have a movable centre which "locks" into place. A later development is to have two gates, technically pound locks, which have a chamber with gates at both ends to control water level. Sluice gates can be moved up and down, thus regulating the flow and level of water, so are

12

principally used for river discharge control (drainage and irrigation). These different types of obstruction can be constructed in combination—all increase the amount of river water.

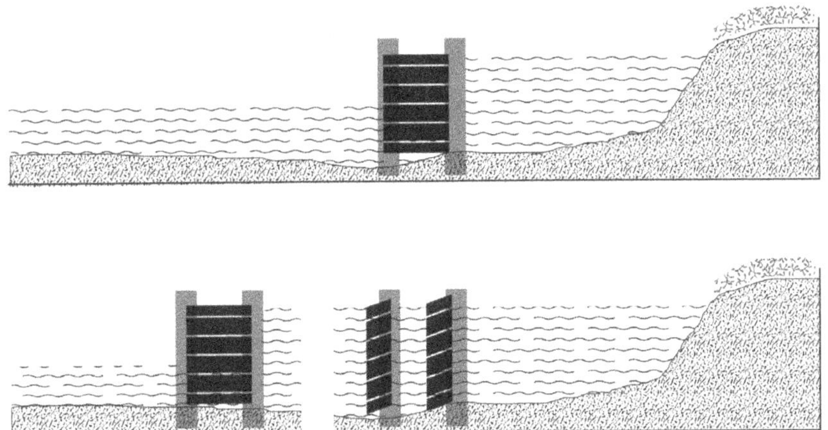

Fig. 10. Sluices control water levels. Runs between sluices can be as long as to the next mill

Plenty of lowland rivers kept much of their water because of their "obstructions" but, for many reasons, have lost it recently (see Fig. 11a, b).

Fig. 11a. River Kennet, Nr Lockeridge (Wiltshire). Winter drought of 2010. After a few years below-average rainfall, except for a few small muddy patches, the river has dried completely

Fig. 11b. A similar Drying Up happened on the River Lavant at Singleton, West Sussex also in winter 2010

Weirs are generally reinstated to improve river ecology and hydromorphology, thus, in the twentieth and twenty-first centuries some are being replaced where it is realised water is too low. **Removing weirs is a form of Drying Up.**

Abstraction also contributes to Drying Up. This may be trivial, just directing off water for a couple of sheep. It may also mean pumping out underground water for a town of hundreds of thousands of people. Cambridge sunk ever-deeper boreholes up to the 1976 drought. After that, the water company sunk the wells to what it considered deep enough—but Development raised its needy head, and to cope with the ever-increasing population, the company now pipes in water from many miles around (even from as far away as Thetford, Norfolk). From 2018 in Britain, abstraction became highly regulated, requiring a licence.

Moving Water About

What happens when all this store is no more? Desalinisation presumably? Reverse Osmosis plants on the coast? There is, so far, sea water in plenty, and if the buildings are in brownfield sites, and do not abstract enough to leave water with too much salt for good marine life, that *is* possible. So is Water Transfer moving water from wetter to drier parts of Britain (north to south,

14

west to east, and, more locally, for example, from the River Cam in Cambridgeshire, south to the River Stour in Suffolk)? This, however, has a great ecological disadvantage: water quality differs between different river types (see Fig. 12a, b, pp. 16–17), and that is before pollution—which also varies—is considered. Polluting a river with, for example, agricultural run-off, **is** pollution. Putting enough nutrient-rich clay river water into pure limestone so that vegetation is altered—that too **is** pollution. Water Transfers do not, in themselves, mean drying up, but since rivers are losing water, yes, the ecosystem is **drying**.

Another cause of river water loss is diversions for infrastructure, for roads and buildings (Fig. 13). In open country, gravity and rock type determine where water gathers and brooks and rivers run. The rain falls the same whether it falls on roads or buildings, but where there is more hard surface, with runoff water that cannot sink into the earth, this means new pathways for the water. These could run straight to existing brooks, but equally could be diverted to concreted channels or to underground pipes which bypass brooks or smaller streams, and carry the water directly to a major river. So smaller watercourses **Dry Up.**

Fig. 13. Stream diverted from original pattern to water the farmhouse and farm; now nearly dry

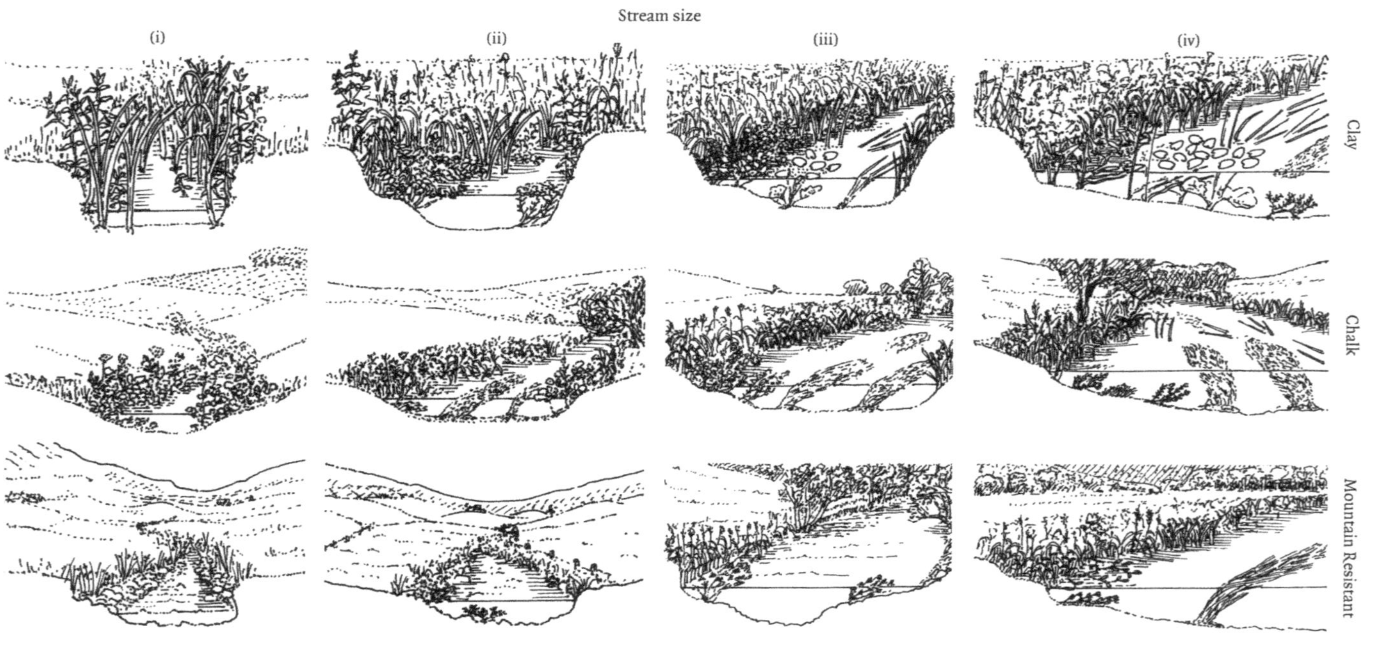

Fig. 12a. Examples of stream sizes and river types. Illustration Y. Bower

16

Fig. 12b. River Types. Illustration Y. Bower

17

Drying Up (and more) **Examples**

Foxton Stream

A good, though simple, example of the collapse of a stream is the Foxton Stream (between the villages of Foxton and Shepreth, Cambridgeshire) a plain ordinary meandering lowland stream, 2–3m wide, in the lowland county of Cambridgeshire. Nothing spectacular—only collapse (Fig. 14). Unfortunately though, only the stream is documented, the plants are not, the stream having gone by the 1970s. Since fish were everywhere, it is likely that fish were in the Foxton Stream, and there could also be watercress and rushes and perhaps waterfowl as useful crops. The most important commodity, though, was the water, pure fresh water, and as the water in the field beside was close to ground level, it was nice and easy to go and collect it with a bucket.

Cows, geese and other creatures had easy access. Presumably because of a potentially good position the stream was diverted here; some houses were built which became the village of Foxton. The early houses had easy access to the stream, and ample water from it. The records are good from the twelfth century, yet another tribute to King Henry the Law Giver, Henry II. Over the next centuries written rules appeared and increased, specifying the width and shape of the stream (good maintenance), when and where water could be removed, washing could be done, and waste emptied into the stream. These rules were complex and, for their date, sensible. They were intended so that all got water, and the water was clean. Unfortunately, if buckets of waste were thrown into the water, that water was not clean, although it may soon have appeared clear, so polluted water spread through the village.

Centuries passed, people, livestock and their water requirement increased, and so did draining of patches of wetland to increase quality yields of pastureland or crops. So, more Drying Up. In the seventeenth century the first well was recorded: not for domestic use, but for industry—malt production. The "Common Stream" had been able to supply the needs of (an expanding) Foxton until now, but this well resulted in over-abstraction. More wells followed in the eighteenth century. Pumps followed. Even this water ran short and was not enough. Water carts appeared, then pipes bringing water from outside. Finally, in the 1970s the drippy remains of the Common Stream, having fed Foxton for a recorded 800 years was put into pipes and the stream bed filled in.

Going, Going, Gone! *No water*, no river. *No water*, no aquatic flora and fauna.

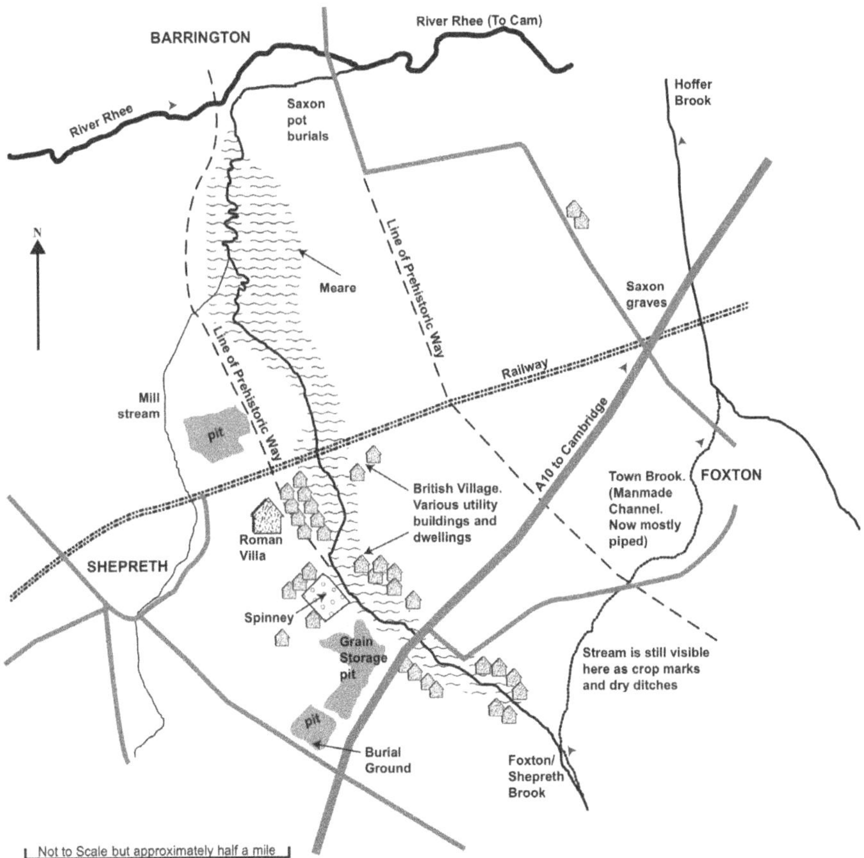

Fig. 14. A stream with no name—which flowed into the R. Rhee. The Foxton Stream was historically a very important waterway as shown in the diagram. In 2018, the stream has mostly been piped underground, and dried. Adapted from Parker, The Common Stream

Obviously the loss of this little brook meant less water flowing into the River Cam. The more "Common" streams were dried and lost, the less water could reach the River Cam, and loss was of stream area, stream volume, plants, eels, fish and so on. Biodiversity and ecological loss.

The Southern Chalkstreams

The once excellent Chalkstreams (rivers) of the south coast—much bigger than the Foxton Stream—have declined also. The Hampshire River Test was renowned for its excellent trout fishery and *Ranunculus* (water crowfoot) vegetation (Fig. 15).

19

Because of the high fees for fishing on the Test, much money could be spent on keeping the river in good condition. The river changed, as rivers always change. In 1930 the riverside grass was partly wetland, and there were plenty of mill weirs. This kept the water level up, and the fish—and plants—in good condition also. By 1970 urban population (so abstraction) was increasing, although because of the weirs and the maintenance, the seriousness was not realised. Later, deterioration meant damage! Patches of brown *Ranunculus* started to appear nearby on the River Avon. It was an unfortunate coincidence that the official reference measurements and records were made **after** this collapse of water and plants.

Fig. 15. A "clean" Chalkstream, River Itchen, Hampshire, September 2011. Clockwise: River vegetation, Ranunculus (Water crowfoot) and wild Brown Trout

In January 2019 the Rivers Test and Itchen were designated "Sites of Special Scientific Interest" (SSSI). The Environment Agency put into place a River Basin Management Plan to protect these waterways, and reviewed abstraction licences and discharge consents.

A 2018 photograph (Fig. 16 River Test) shows that *Ranunculus* is growing well but is all squashed together. There are indeed plenty of well-growing leafy shoots, but where is the habitat for the animals? It is not available in the same way as historically, the space is just not there. Of course there are still habitats which have plenty of water and animals, but they are now few. Too often the botanist says, "Ah, *Ranunculus*, water crowfoot is there so all is well". It is in fact important to look more deeply. It is indeed important to have the *Ranunculus*—but for a good habitat, much more is needed.

Fig. 16. Ranunculus penicillatus *growing well but in "cramped" conditions, indicating lack of water*

Constable's paintings of the River Avon are approximately 200 years old, and the one showing the water plants best shows the water crowfoot stems spread out throughout the river (Fig. 17a). Each stem has plenty of oxygen and water chemicals around it, so it can grow well. The network is spread out enough for small fish to swim through freely, and invertebrates to live and grow.

By the 1970s came loss of water, failure of vegetation, failure of trout. Looking just at the water in the river, the water was still clear and moving well: but it had "tipped over". Abstraction and damage had done their work, but done it imperceptibly, so it is only by, for instance, looking at the Constable picture of the River Avon at Salisbury and comparing it with virtually the same scene *c.* 1970 (Fig. 17b) that the full extent of water loss is realised. We cannot be sure just from these pictures, but it appears that the meadows are now wetter (lower level) and the river shallower, and reedbeds have gone.

Fig. 17a. John Constable's Salisbury Cathedral, from the Meadows, c. 1830 shows ample water. The horses legs are almost submerged

Fig. 17b. Appears to be the same scene, c. 1970, and shows the water level at only ankle deep around the cows (Adapted from photograph by Antony Miles)

In 2012, The Angling Trust wrote,

"We are privileged in this country, to have most of the world's Chalkstreams. We have abused that privilege, by abstracting, polluting and damaging these unique rivers so that they support a fraction of the life that they should."

The Houghton Fishing Club is famously very private, and has a restricted, elected membership of a mere 25. It was founded in 1822 and owns 13 miles of the bank of the River Test. Recently its members managed to persuade the EU to pay costs for three years to reverse the river's deterioration—but it is asking much to reverse a century of mismanagement in just three years.

In fact 2012 had exceptionally high rainfall, and many rivers, including these Chalkstreams, had a short-term revival. River plants not seen for years reappeared in a surprising number of places.

Just as temporary wet years (by bringing more water) can have a marked effect, so can temporary dry ones. However (as fully discussed in Haslam, *River Plants of Western Europe, The River Scene,* and *The Waving Plants of the River*, Appendix III), river plants are very sensitive to water depth, within their specific range. Over that depth the plants grow well, unless and until they are limited by lack of light. Under their preferred depth there is the peculiar and so far unexplained phenomenon of Shallow Death (Fig. 18), where water volume, oxygen, and other growing conditions are sufficient (though methane has not been tested), but water-supported plants still die. (Emergents are unaffected, as long as liquid water is present.)

So temporary water loss is a warning of what will happen permanently with more **Drying Up**.

Small brooks in a drought and the vegetation

Several hundred brooks about 2–6m wide were surveyed before, during and after the 1976 drought, mostly from ridges of low lowland hills, for example, the Lincolnshire Wolds. The data record a temporary water loss, which is the same as the start of a permanent loss, and in that instance the changes recorded here would have had an unhappy instead of a happy ending—the collapse would have been permanent.

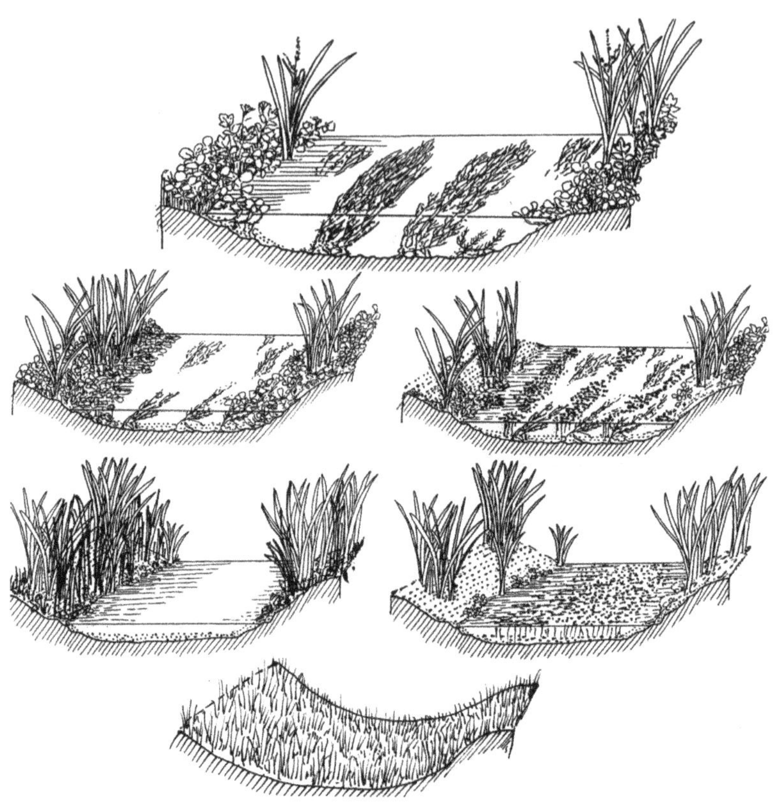

Fig. 18. Shallowing sequence from normal (top) to dried. More pollution on right.
Illustration by Y Bower

An aquatic plant species has a depth range in which it can develop well, a peripheral range in which it is more easily eliminated by other factors, and a further range in which it cannot grow. If a 15–20cm change in water level keeps within the depth range for good growth, a species will remain unchanged, unless, for instance, shallower water allows tall "monocots" (Monocotyledons are grass-like, reed-like, sedge-like vegetation) to dominate, and to suppress shorter species. If, however, a 15–20cm change in depth means that the species is in a less favourable depth, it may decline. Consequently, it is not just the actual change which is important, but the change in relation to the water-depth bands of the particular species. During the 1976 drought, where the water depth dropped from over 20cm to 20cm and under, 10% of the sites with water starwort, *Callitriche* spp., and 25% of those with water crowfoot, *Ranunculus* spp., lost these species. Where water depth dropped from over 40cm to below 20cm, 50% of sites with strapweed, *Sparganium emersum*, lost that species.

24

As a brook dries, the above-ground parts of water-supported species usually die first. However, there are exceptions: plants last longer on damp soil and, for example, *Callitriche* spp. can have aerial forms in winterbournes. Falling water levels leave parts of banks dry, so affect plant-colonisation patterns.

During drought, there may be fewer or no storm flows. Storm flows increase scour in the river bed and, by raising the water level above the normal level, the water both floods and scours plants on the lower bank. Storm flows generally scour more in the upper than in the lower reaches of a river, so the effect of drought is shown where plants could grow in 1976 on sites from which they would be washed away in other years.

Fringing herbs showed little change in streams where they can always anchor well, for example, lowland Chalk ones. In the hills, and in lowland streams with less stable flows that affected the edges, fringing herbs, because of the new stability, increased substantially in frequency and diversity at individual sites. Badly anchored water-supported species increased similarly, particularly in the (ordinarily) less-stable lowland streams, like clay streams with mild pollution, where rooting ability and so anchorage had been decreased (e.g., *Callitriche* spp. and *Elodea canadensis*, Canadian pond weed).

In the lowlands, there was a minor increase in those species which are easily pulled away by swifter flows, for example *Callitriche* spp.. In hill streams, where water force is usually much higher, having less rain and fewer storms was much more significant. During the 1976 drought, *Elodea canadensis*, *Ranunculus* spp., and blanket weed in particular, grew well in upstream brooks where they had previously been absent or scarce. The absence of storm scour allowed not just growth, but good growth, of these plants. (Blanket weed is an ephemeral plant with a swift life cycle—so a very quick response time in such streams—whilst the flowering plants develop much more slowly). Where well-moving water is required for good growth (*Ranunculus* for example), those species declined during the drought. Small changes in flow can, therefore, increase or decrease the quantity and the species of river plants when the changes move outside the preferred habitat band of the species.

Sedimentation increases with decreased flow. With silt deposited, species including *Callitriche* spp., *Elodea canadensis*, *Groenlandia densa* (opposite-leaved pondweed) and *Zannichellia palustris* (horned pondweed) can invade, until the silt—along with the plants—is washed out again in a spate. The tall monocot, *Sparganium erectum*, can increase in small streams with silting and low flows, forming edge bands that shade and smother smaller species. (A collapse? Not in quantity, but in diversity and community.)

Brooks which had dried for one year kept a fair diversity of fringing herbs and tall monocotyledons. However, brooks that were dried for over two years were usually covered by grasses or other land plants, perhaps with sparse fringing herbs or reedgrass (*Phalaris arundinacea*). In summer-dry brooks, silt retains water longer than gravel. Where gravel in winterbournes bears, for example, unhealthy fools cress (*Apium nodiflorum*) and land plants, silt may have several fringing herbs, aerial *Callitriche* spp. and *Ranunculus* spp.. *Apium nodiflorum* extends further into dry brooks, but was lost from *c.* 30% of sites dry for over a year. Brook lime (*Veronica beccabunga*), then edible watercress (*Rorippa nasturtium-aquaticum* agg.) were lost from about half the brook sites which were dry for over a year. Bur-reed (*Sparganium erectum*), though, was lost from less than 25%, and from even fewer, if the fringes were dry, and the brook centre was flooded.

Fringing herbs decreased in dried lowland brooks, but increased elsewhere, giving a net increase mostly in middle and upper non-Chalkstreams, primarily because of the shallowing and lack of storm flows washing away clumps. Exposing more habitat was secondary. The increase in fringing herbs in hill streams was mainly due to lack of storm flow, but partly due to more silting and so better development. Two or three years later, fringing herbs were nearly back to normal except for their great increase in those lowland brooks not yet having normal storm flows.

Tall monocots likewise increased in the lowlands, and because they are less easy to wash out than fringing herbs, and profited from the extra silting, they persisted longer after the drought.

In the lowlands, water-supported species decreased, as noted above, though blanket weed, which can grow in very little water, decreased the least. In the hills, there was no net change (shallower water had losses; places with lower water force had gains).

River Chelmer, Essex

River Chelmer is on lowland clay, so it is as nutrient-rich as any English river, and because there are no winterbournes, there are no upstream ecotypes which tolerate and recover quickly from drying. The downstream vegetation is typical, and more nutrient-rich than that of most European rivers. (A small drop in water level here would have little effect, as the difference between 1.5m and 1.75m is negligible for those species.) There was no collapse here.

Upstream, however, shallowing from the 1976 drought made a significant difference, causing shortage of water-supported species. The stream recovered well within three years. The more limestone the lowland stream, the quicker the recovery from this drought. A pure clay stream like the River Chelmer recovered the slowest, so there was a collapse upstream, but only a temporary one.

The 1976 and 1992 droughts were just temporary droughts, nothing serious. If, though, the fall in water level had been through drainage and abstraction and was prolonged, then the upper streams would have permanently lost their water plants. As indeed happened with the *c.* 2000 collapse (which may yet, of course, show recovery)! Water-supported species are lost first, the tougher emergents persist longer. For instance, if the stream beds remain damp, the aquatics will still die, but a wetland vegetation will develop over as much of the bed as is not scoured by storm flows. Upstream, beyond where there was perennial water, there were dry stream beds, well sunk (i.e. dredged and drained) with sparse or patchy land and wetland plants. Such streams, given more time and no dredging, gradually fall into disuse (outside major storms) and become channels in land vegetation.

River Cam, Cambridgeshire

Finally, a fully documented, very rare, example—not just of water loss, but also of other damage. This is from central Cambridge regarding the River Cam, its associated ditches, streams and other watercourses, ponds and pools, which dates from 1660! There can be unexpected gains in having a stable and excellent University, with interested Botanists, in a city!

The original Cambridge records show 62 aquatics present, 22 of which are now thought to be extinct. One-third of the species in about 350 years lost (various records from elsewhere fit in with this, though are less well documented).

In the early nineteenth century, as common in many towns, sewage was allowed in the river. As sewage waste further increased, no other means of disposal was found, so it still went into the river. (In the mists of time this also happened, of course, in Cambridge, but as the town expanded with more human waste, it was stopped.) In the mid-Victorian age it was recognised that this meant unpleasantness, awful smells **and** disease and inevitably the loss of river plants. Such sewage differed greatly from today's effluent. Firstly, it was untreated. This meant there was much solids (early human waste was only sewage) and a lower variety of pollutants. Hard surface runoff dirtied by traffic was trivial, and so were all the household chemicals of the time, including toothpaste and medicines, which increasingly have altered the behaviour of too many river animals (see the Book in this Series entitled *WATER: Clean and Dirty*). So, over time, very high organic content and oxygen-absorbing chemicals have been removed at sewage treatment works, but there are still many toxins at very low levels (for example, a few parts per billion or trillion) which damage the ecology and are not removed by the treatment.

Lost before 1860: Lesser water plantain—(*Baldellia ranunculoides* formerly *B. palustris*), Bog bean (*Menyanthes trifoliatus*), and Grass-wrack-leaved pondweed (*Potamogeton compressus* formerly *P. zosterifolius*).

Lost before 1912: Mares tail (*Hippuris palustris* formerly *H. vulgaris* L.), Water crowfoot (*Ranunculus aquatilis)*, Frog bit (*Hydrocharis morsus-ranae*), Fine-leaved water dropwort (*Oenanthe aquatica* formerly *Phellandium aquaticum*), Tubular water dropwort (*Oenanthe fistulosa*), Slender sedge/Woolly fruited sedge (*Carex lasiocarpa*) and Water horsetail (*Equisetum fluviatile*).

Common species in 2014: Kingcup, Marsh marigold (*Caltha palustris*) (Fig. 19a), Lesser spearwort (*Ranunculus flammula*), Celery-leaved water crowfoot (*Ranunculus sceleratus*), Round-leaved water crowfoot (*Ranunculus omiophyllus*), Brackish water crowfoot (*Ranunculus baudotii*), Water mint (*Mentha aquatica*), Six-stamened Waterwort (*Elatine hexandra)*, Blue water speedwell (*Veronica anagallis-aquatica*), Pink water speedwell (*Veronica catenata*), Flowering Rush (*Butomus umbellatus*) (Fig. 19b).

The Cambridge records show that wide-leaved *Potamogetons*, once found whenever there was good water space, were lost when intensive management came to the rivers (as also happened on the European continent). Even though some species such as fennel pondweed (*Potamogeton pectinatus*) have enormous numbers of turions (small specialised vegetative buds which spread over the river bed), heavy machinery—plus the decreasing water—over a period of time wipes out the large *Potamogetons*. Machine-digging, plus tearing up rhizomes, weakens and eventually kills the species.

Oenanthe fluviatilis persisted longer than the other *Oenanthe* spp. whose numbers dropped sharply only after 1950. Ecologically this aquatic plant occurs where silt or clay mixes with Chalk or other soft limestone, especially when a weir holds up muddy water. So, is cleaning bad?

Pondweeds, because of their name, were presumably once abundant, as were field and village ponds in which they grew. In the 1930s, all types were so. By the 1970s, fine-leaved species were much sparser, though wide-leaved ones (especially the pollution-favouring *Potamogeton pectinatus*) occurred frequently. By 2010, even the wide-leaved species were sparse, including the earlier-profuse *P. pectinatus*.

Fig. 19a. Kingcup, Marsh marigold (Caltha palustris)

Fig. 19b. Flowering Rush (Butomus umbellatus)

Discussion

Many aquatic plants have decreased in number, and it is not easy to draw proven conclusions as to why this has happened. Given the general and deplorable losses over most of the country, detail is difficult. The River Cam data are comprehensive, and show that water violet (*Hottonia palustris*) is one of the species which has become extinct over the surveyed area. However, within some 50m of that original boundary, water violet re-appeared in a watercourse in the 1990s. Very close! Extinct? Present? Persistent?

Similarly, it is possible for a river to be channelled, and lose all species, but after perhaps 30 years, the sides start to fall in, and water plants [re]colonize. Nevertheless, generally, what used to be a river full of its characteristic species is now one with a plant perhaps every *c.* 50m, different to the previous ones, and without tributaries. No water, no water plants.

Some species decrease because of very clear causes. Others may also have several obvious causes, for example, water level reduced by half, swan numbers increased, public walking along bank paths increased. Other causes may be far from clear: obvious pollution, or channelling, many canoes? In what proportion are losses due to each cause—both obvious or obscure?

Those who were involved in the floods of 2012–14 in Britain will remember vividly what it was like to have saturated soil, with water moving, gently or violently, downhill. This is how it once was, all over Britain, including in the green fields. How many noticed during those floods that arable fields (except where flooding occurred normally) did not in fact look quite so sodden, and did they wonder why? The reason for this is that most of the (non-hill or "wild" country) is underdrained, it has sub-surface pipes with holes in, or channels with tiles ready to drain off incoming rain! Whilst underdrainage was known and practised centuries ago, like with main drainage, it was the impetus of the Victorians that both improved and spread it widely, to improve crop yield. Field drainage has numerous small drains running parallel with each other downstream through the fields which discharge into streams or ditches. Much was done when the fields were laid out post-Enclosure Act. Even since 1945 field drainage has improved, the sopping clay-mud at the downstream side of clay or semi-clay fields being drained off quicker (see Figs 20 and 21).

Underdrainage has been so effective that irrigation is now often needed in dry periods—not just during drought, but also in ordinary dry periods expected every English summer. Irrigation (rather than plant breeding for crops to withstand mild drought) is wasting water left on the land after drainage by putting it back onto the land (Fig. 22).

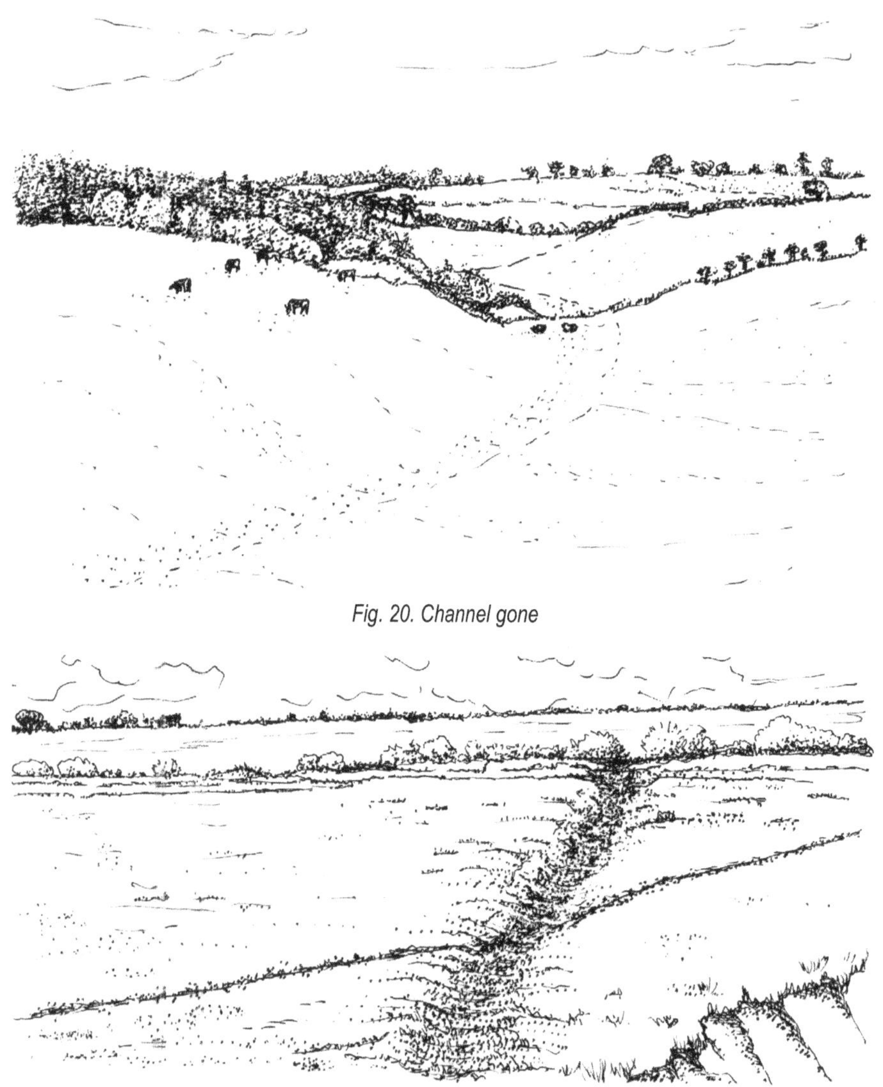

Fig. 20. Channel gone

Fig. 21. Former stream diverted to straight field-edge ditch, dried

It is now recognized that wasting water in this way is not viable, and removal of river water for irrigation is now restricted. To counteract these restrictions, more farmers are creating reservoirs to catch winter rainfall to use in summer.

Fig. 22. Typical large-scale Linear and Pivot irrigation system, Norfolk, c. 2015

This is sensible, although it is not so sensible as arranging the drainage to leave some water in the fields, and breeding crops to tolerate ordinary summer drying. Looking at aerial photographs of lowland England shows time and again, region after region, that old streams wander across the fields on their way to the stream at the base of the slope. When these fields were first laid out, these streams were inefficient for drainage as they were too few, too meandering, with too-slow flow. They were replaced by ditches surrounding the fields which carried the water that had been in the now-lost streams, draining out of over-saturated soils in winter, draining slowly and often still wet in summer.

The lost streams were, of course, aquatic habitat, bearing wetland and aquatic plants as appropriate, and associated animals. Remember that historically a great economic asset to a manor was the fowl it provided. Then there were fish, and it is surprising how eels can live in very small rills (and of course they can travel across wet land). All these increased biodiversity, which, sadly, is now much reduced.

In drought, the harder parts and reproductive parts of plants may well survive, the seedbank may not. River beds vary from rock (few seeds!), stones, gravel, sand (and mixes), through which water drains, to clay, which holds water and can keep plant parts alive for months. Prolonged drying, by whatever cause, leads to death, as is all too clearly seen, for example, in Malta (Tropical Agriculture Association (TAA), *Agriculture for Development*), whose surface water has all but disappeared, and fresh water is now produced by desalination plants. Garigue (dry southern heathland) is a beautiful and fascinating sight: but not when it is growing on the bottom of what was once a river!

When streams were converted into ditches the length might have increased (where streams crossing a field were replaced by four ditches going round it to improve drainage). But these ditches were more "ditch-shaped" with steep uniform sides, so with far fewer plants and animals (Figs 2, 3b). Water habitat remained, but it was less, ecologically, and had less water heritage. Yet water heritage remained. Hedging-and-ditching used to be a normal occupation on the land in winter to keep the fields dry enough for good crops.

With field drainage came a further lowering of the water table. The land dried. Water level fell below ditch level for most of the year. Ditches mostly lost their water, apart from storm drainage flow, and aquatic habitat was lost. A mainly dry ditch, not cleared out too often, may still bear, for example *Filipendula ulmaria* (Meadowsweet). A dried one is empty or with land plants. This is the loss of aquatic habitat in farmland.

Small streams and ditches gather water into larger ones, which eventually become sizeable streams, brooks, or rivers.

It is not just cropland which is drained. Most wet land has at some time been considered for drainage, and much if it has been more or less drained at times. There are low flood plains to fill lakes, and high moorlands and heaths— though lakes can be high, and heaths low, and raised bogs can develop over both.

Since the ice of the last Ice Age some 8,000 years ago retreated from the lowlands, the flats of eastern England (ex-Rhône flood plain) have risen and fallen (see Table 1). When the Fens became drier, with a greater population which needed to be fed, ground water was further drained by constructing channels, and the drained land could then be farmed. When neither occurred, the Fens reverted to, well, fen (with some marsh, bog, wet woodland and open water). Because peat oxidises away when exposed, the Fens, like for example, part of The Netherlands, are now below ground level. Bigger and deeper channels, with pumps, drain more. Fenland Water levels are now maintained by pumps and sluices, with Denver Sluice being the main holder-in of the sea. Historical changes to the Denver Sluice since it was first constructed were succinctly summarised by G.E. Matthews in 1929: *"The changes in Denver Sluice...: Built, 1652; Improved, 1682; Blew up, 1713; Rebuilt by C. Labelye, 1750; Reconstructed by John Rennie, 1832; Enlarged, 1923."*

In 2019 it is known as the "Denver Complex" and consists of several well-placed sluices which control water flow to protect the Fenland, much of which is below sea level, from both sea incursion and river flood.

Table 1. Climate and geomorphic changes in the Fenland

1900	Becoming dry and intensely cultivated
1650	The Drainage of the Fens (more intermittent than would appear from the simple literature)
Mediaeval, Early Modern	Some drainage, particularly in drier eras
Anglo-Saxon	Huge fens
Roman	Man-made watercourses, drainage
Iron Age	Build-up of silt, giving the present division of Silt and Peat Fens
1000 BC to AD 0	Sea incursion, extensive waterlogging, open sedge fen
To *c.* 2000 BC	Sea level drop, freshwater fen spread, and fen passing via carr to wood Peat increase, trees invaded from the margin. Raised bog developing where alkaline flooding least (Middle Fens, and fen edge)
c. 2500–2000 BC	A vast brackish lagoon, 1–2 m deep. coastal silt deposited, followed by *Phragmites* then inland sedge and woods far inland
c. 2500 BC	Rapid peat development, sedge fen, recent black peat. Sedge fen leading to carr then woods
c. 3000 BC	Sea incursion, waterlogged, freshwater ponded inland. Black peat developed in this
4000–3000 BC	Dry acid peat, south fens remained alkaline, middle, to raised bog (only marginally affected by fen clay)

The first successful drainage of the Fenland in the late fifteenth and early sixteenth centuries (earlier, the Romans tried but failed!), concentrated the aquatic habitat into drainage channels and so the loss was of wetland, not of aquatic habitat. As the channels became deeper below ground level, with steep and inhospitable sides and shallower or with no water, aquatics were lost.

Maps—Ordnance Survey (OS) or other good maps—mark rivers. They also mark smaller watercourses. But how is it decided what size of stream should be marked on a map or what water is shown?

The *c.* 1900 OS 6-inches-to-the-mile maps were carefully and fully surveyed. Those with water at that time are marked. Since then, there has been no general mapping of water, but much loss of water. In the 1970s, typical highland streams had permanent running water, well upstream of where water is marked on the OS maps. Drainage had been little since *c.* 1900 (although it soon followed). On the other hand, in the farming lowlands, field and main drainage had really taken effect, and generally the upper marked stretches of watercourses were dry, covered by land plants, or empty, and perennial water started well downstream. So, just in this short 70 years, ground water level dropped by 30–50cm.

The widespread phenomenon of Shallow Death has not attracted the interest of physiologists. The water is shallower than the normal range, whatever that may be. Yet there is ample water for the development of, for instance, *Potamogeton crispus* (curled pondweed), growing with really quite flat shoots (in faster flow), and 30–50cm in depth. If most of the water is removed so the brook becomes 25cm deep, the plant fails to grow and fades away. Experiments have shown that if the plant is put in a growth chamber where the water level never drops, it will still fade and die in shallower water. Many other species react in the same way. As a stream dries, more of its water-supported species are in over-shallow water. Frail-leaved submerged plants are usually lost first.

The emergents, the plants which grow above water anyway, grow in shallower water, partly because they reach from soil to air, so cannot span a lengthy range of water, partly because growing up in the air to survive, they must stand up, not flop, as a water-supported plant would do. They therefore tend to be found on fringes and islands. They do not usually suffer from Shallow Death. Certainly wetland aquatics require water, but most can live happily with their shoots mainly in the air for some years (see Table 2). Each species has a different range and these are generalisations.

Looking at a river in otherwise good condition, there should be plenty of water-supported species across the river and of emergents on the fringes. If the river has plenty of emergents, but the water-supported species are few (and the water is obviously not too deep) this is (usually) **Shallowing**.

Table 2. The Importance of River Water Depths to Common Aquatic Plants

WATER DEPTH / *species peaking in*	up to 30cm		30–75cm		75–120cm		Over 120cm		Unimportant
	Very	*Slightly*	*Very*	*Slightly*	*Very*	*Slightly*	*Very*	*Slightly*	
Agrostis stolonifera									+
Alisma plantago-aquatica		+							
Apium nodiflorum	+								
Berula erecta	+								
Butomus umbellatus							+		
Callitriche spp.			+						
Carex acutiformis agg.				+					
Ceratophyllum demersum				+		+			
Elodea canadensis				+		+			
Glyceria maxima		+							
Lemna minor agg.									+
Mentha aquatica		+							
Myosotis scorpioides		+							
Myriophyllum spicatum						+			
Nuphar lutea								+	
Petasites hybridus			+						
Thalaris arundinacea						+			
Phragmites australis		+							
Polygonum amphibium						+			
Potamogeton crispus									+
Potamogeton natans		+		+					
Potamogeton pectinatus						+			
Ranunculus spp.			+		+				
Rorippa amphibia						+		+	
Rorippa nasturium-aquaticum agg.	+								
Rumex hydrolapathum								+	
Sagittaria sagittifolia								+	
Scirpus lacustris								+	
Sparganium emersum						+			
Sparganium erectum					+				
Typha latifolia		+							
Veronica anagallis-aquatica agg.		+							
Veronica beccabunga	+								
Zannichellia palustris				+					
Mosses (aggregated)	+								
Blanket Weed				+					

England's Largest Wetlands

The two largest English wetlands, historically, are those of East Anglia (Fenland, Norfolk Broads) and Somerset (the Levels and Moors). Looking at photographs from the 1840s onwards is instructive. Pictures of the Fenland start as flat lands, broken by dykes and farmsteads (with clumps of poplars, giving some shelter and some break-up of the uniform landscape). There is no doubt this is a harsh riverscape, foggy, icy in winter, damp throughout the year (with much low-lying mist obscuring views), saturated: with pumps (steam-powered changing to electric-powered) working most of the time. The level of the fields and dykes is well below that of the rivers: an obvious and indeed startling reminder of the wetland and the drying. Flooding is now usually minor, as—by the twentieth century—drainage was very efficient, and most of the excess rainwater was diverted and pumped up into the rivers, and thence conducted to the sea, via heavily embanked channels. This degree of soil loss (drying, oxygenation, disappearance) is not found in the other wetlands, where rivers are only rather above, or indeed at present soil level.

The bareness, uniformity and bleakness of these wetlands was great. By the 1970s the land was much drier, and some hedges and (mostly planted) trees were large enough to be prominent. By 1990, the Fenland was dry enough for hedges instead of, or as well as, dykes, and by 2010 large trees and well-grown hedges had broken up the riverscape, which while of course still flat, was (in good weather!) no longer bleak. In the Somerset Levels, again the drier parts had good hedges, but fewer full-grown trees. Drying Up, indeed, and a major change in landscape, prominent dykes, and woody growth within one lifetime.

Whilst hedges replaced dykes, what happened to the aquatic habitat with its huge flora and fauna?

Well, as usual, no water, no water animals or plants….

REFERENCES

Haslam, S.M. *The Waving Plants of the River*. 2013. Forrest Text, Cardigan. 278 pp. ISBN 978-0-9564692-4-3.

Haslam, S.M. *River Plants of Western Europe*. 2nd Edition. 2006. Forrest Text, Cardigan. 438 pp. ISBN 09550740 4 5.

Haslam, S.M. *The River Scene: Ecology and Cultural Heritage*. 1997. Cambridge University Press. 344 pp. ISBN 0-521-57410-2.

Haslam, S.M. 1987. *River Plants of Western Europe*. Cambridge University Press. 512 pp. ISBN 0-521-26427-8.

Matthews, G.E. "The drainage of the fens and marshlands of the Wash", *Journal Institution Municipal and County Engineers*. 1929. p. 443.

Natural Environment Research Council (NERC). 2019 [Accessed 2 August 2019]: https://nerc.ukri.org/research/funded/programmes/droughts/.

Parker, R. *The Common Stream*. 1975. William Collins Sons & Co. Ltd. Glasgow. 283 pp. ISBN 0 00 216113 3.

Tropical Agriculture Association. Bone, T. "Fresh water and crops in Malta". In, TAA UK, *Newsletter* (now *Agriculture for Development*), pp. 25–29, June 2001. 40pp., ISSN 1759-0604 (Print), ISSN 1759-0612 (Online URL: https://taa.org.uk/wp-content/uploads/2018/10/JuneNewsletter2001.pdf.

THE RIVER FRIEND SERIES

This series of small books is designed for people with a general or specific interest in rivers.
Please visit the River Friend Website for an up to-date list of
PUBLISHED Titles: **http://www.riverfriend.tinasfineart.uk /home**

Standalone Titles in the Series include:

A PROLOGUE TO THE SERIES: Plant identification and Glossary of Terms
(ISBN 978 1 9162096 2 6)

DRYING UP (ISBN 978 1 9162096 1 9)

STREAM STORY I: A Riveting Riverscape—River Brue, Somerset
(ISBN 978 1 9162096 0 2)

INTERPRET: What do Plants Tell us? (ISBN 978 1 9162096 5 7)

Vegetation Changes Over Time. Is there FREEZE FRAME?
(ISBN 978 1 9162096 6 4)

REED—ON THE EDGE (ISBN 978 1 9162096 4 0)

An Introduction to the WATER FRAMEWORK DIRECTIVE
(ISBN 978 1 9162096 3 3)

WATER: Clean and Dirty (ISBN 978 1 9162096 7 1)

STREAM STORY II: A Brook in Transit: Bourn Brook, Cambs
(ISBN 978 1 9162096 8 8)

CHANGE: What a Disaster! (ISBN 978 1 9162096 9 5)

LOOK AT THE BOTTOM

How to lose Fresh Water in Under Two Centuries. The Example of MALTA

VEGETATION PATTERNS

IN THE WATER

THE WATERS OF WELLS

RESTORE, REHABILITATE, IMPROVE

AWFUL ALIENS

About the Authors

Sylvia Haslam is a botanist and river culture, etc., specialist. Anyone wanting to find out more should look at the publications list on her website (http://www.riversandreeds.co.uk). Her publications specific to this series are listed in the book entitled *A PROLOGUE TO THE SERIES: Plant identification and Glossary of Terms*.

Tina Bone has worked as a self-employed Desktop Publisher for many years until she changed career to work as a Professional Artist from March 2005. To view Tina's resumé and artwork please visit her website: http://www.tinasfineart.uk.